Labour's Forgotten Statement
on
Banking and Finance

Introduced by
J. E. Mortimer

SPOKESMAN
for
SOCIALIST RENEWAL

Labour's forgotten statement on Banking and Finance

J. E. Mortimer

In the discussion within the labour movement and the press about the current failings of the financial system, the 'credit crunch' and the consequential rise in unemployment little, if any, attention has been given to a statement entitled 'Banking and Finance', prepared by the National Executive Committee of the Labour Party and then presented to and accepted by the 1976 annual conference of the Party.

The report saw the operation of Britain's financial system within the wider context of the problems of the economy. How right they were! At the heart of these problems was the need to increase industrial investment. This need, said the Labour Party report, was 'too important to be left to businessmen and financiers alone'. The report called for a doubling of the rate of manufacturing investment over the next decade. Manufacturing, it said, had 'grown anaemic and needed a major transformation'.

The Labour Party's statement argued that the funds to pay for such a massive expansion of manufacturing investment could not come solely from ploughed back profits or even from a strengthened National Enterprise Board. A larger proportion of long-term funds would have to come from outside sources such as banks and other financial institutions. Hence it was essential to examine the flow of funds to ensure that industry had the necessary degree of support.

This warning from the Labour Party was in large measure disregarded. Manufacturing continued to shrink and soothing words were used about the growth of financial services and the services sector. The Labour Party made proposals for the extension of social ownership and fundamental changes in policy.

In subsequent years, the housing policy, associated above all with Mrs Thatcher, worsened the situation. Council house building for rent declined at a steep rate. All the emphasis was on the growth of home ownership, with ever-increasing debt. The assumption was that the debt would be met by the ever-increasing prices of property, providing so-called 'gains in capital equity'. When the bubble burst, we all became familiar with the term 'subprime mortgages'. The downturn started in the United States and spread rapidly to many other countries, including Britain.

Unfortunately, the Labour Party's 1976 statement on 'Banking and Finance' was not adopted as a guide by New Labour when it was elected with an overwhelming majority in 1997. There is a lesson in this experience.

Banking and Finance

FOREWORD

The 1971 Annual Conference committed the National Executive Committee to bringing forward proposals for public ownership of the banks, insurance companies and building societies. Arising from this decision the National Executive Committee set up a Study Group to explore the detailed practical considerations involved. The report of this Study Group was published in August 1973 as an Opposition Green Paper.

The NEC's Home Policy Committee subsequently assumed direct responsibility for work on banking and insurance, and asked its Housing Policy Sub-Committee to examine the role played by non-profit-making building societies in the light of their obvious relevance to solving our housing problems. Proposals on building society mortgage finance were included in evidence submitted to the Government's current review of housing finance, and in Labour's Programme 1976.

Following the decision of the 1975 Annual Conference to remit Composite 34 (moved by AUEW-TASS, seconded by COHSE), the Home Policy Committee was able to complete its studies on banking and insurance with two special meetings held in early 1976. It is in the light of these detailed studies that the National Executive Committee commends this Statement to Conference.

August 1976

RON HAYWARD
GENERAL SECRETARY

"Virtually no corner of the City has emerged from the past twelve months unscathed. The secondary banks have been decimated, and the Bank of England and the clearing banks are still labouring under a rescue operation that has been transformed from the comparatively simple task of recycling liquid funds to the secondary banks to the far more onerous job of propping up fundamentally weak fringe institutions. At the same time the crisis of confidence and liquidity has spread far further than anyone could have guessed, to engulf some of the leading finance houses . . .

Even the insurance industry, for so long a bastion of security, had its problems. Difficulties of Nation Life, Welfare Insurance and London Indemnity & General forced all investors to think again about just how safe their savings were".

(From 'The City—Annual Survey' in
"The Banker" February 1975).

.

Introduction

1. The operations of the UK financial system have long been of concern to the Labour Movement. In our statement to the 1975 Party Conference "Labour and Industry" we accepted that industrial and economic planning must be supported by a coherent framework of financial planning, and explained that we were studying various ways in which both the banks and other financial institutions could make a more positive contribution to increasing industrial investment.

2. In the light of those studies it is clear that the investment expansion Britain desperately needs is too important to be left to businessmen and financiers alone. We need to adopt an economic strategy which is founded on an understanding that:—

* The heart of Britain's weakness lies in its comparatively poor record of investment, especially in manufacturing industry which has grown anaemic as a result and needs a major transfusion amounting to a doubling of the rate of manufacturing investment over the next decade. This is the target we must set.

* The funds to pay for such a massive expansion of manufacturing investment cannot come just from ploughed back profits, or even from a beefed-up National Enterprise Board. Companies must therefore break with the old habits that have reduced Britain to one of Europe's poor relations. They must look to outside sources like the banks and other financial institutions for a larger proportion of the long-term funds they need, as do their major European and Japanese competitors.

* Hence an examination of corporate finance and the flow of funds within the economy is essential: to find new ways of mobilising companies' internal funds, and to ensure that British industry has the degree of positive support from the finance system required for the achievement of national economic objectives.

3. It is this last point to which this Statement is directed. Its objects are five-fold:—

(1) To indicate the pattern of saving and investment within the UK economy and how it compares with that of our main competitors.

(2) To explain the extent to which their position as intermediaries—channelling funds from savers and depositors to borrowers and investors—has put into the hands of the banks and other financial institutions a vast concentration of private power.

(3) To call into serious question the way in which the banks and financial institutions have met their responsibilities to their customers, and to suggest that by short-term and short-sighted lending and investment policies they have undermined the development of the national economy.

(4) To note the contribution which public ownership within the financial system has made to the success of some of our major foreign competitors, and its relevance not only to giving further expression to our socialist philosophy, but also to the practical and immediate problem of regenerating British industry.

(5) To present a set of proposals which constitute a thorough-going reform of the financial system, giving the Government a dominant influence, though not monopoly control, over its detailed operations and investment policies.

Company Finance, Investment and Saving

Investment

4. Britain's average rate of economic growth lags well behind our main rivals. It is clear that a major part of the explanation lies in our poor investment record. The evidence also suggests that we have been dropping even further behind since the late 1960's.

5. At the beginning of the 1970's Britain devoted less than two-thirds the share of her Gross Domestic Product to investment compared to France and West Germany—18 per cent by Britain, 28 per cent by her two European neighbours (Source: OECD Financial Statistics). Over the whole period 1960-72 *manufacturing investment* as a percentage of Gross Domestic Product averaged 3.8 in Britain compared with 4.9 in West Germany, 6.9 in France and 8.9 in Japan (Sources: Mainly OECD National Accounts, quoted in NEDO 'Finance for Investment' Table 2.4).

6. Estimates made by the independent Bank for International Settlements of the average annual increase in national output attributable to investment show the following:—

	1962-67 %	1967-72 %
UK	0.60	0.33
West Germany	0.70	1.00
France	1.90	1.60

(Source: BIS Annual Report 1972/73 page 7, quoted in Samuels, Groves and Goddard 'Company Finance in Europe' page 324).

7. The marked decline in fixed investment in 1971-3 coincided with substantial increases in gross company profits and with annual increases in retained profits (after adjustment for stock appreciation) of about 30 per cent (Source: NEDO op cit Table 4.1). Figures such as these show, at the very least, how unreliable an increase in company profits can be as a guide to future investment. But they go far to explain Edward Heath's exasperated cry to the Institute of Directors in 1973:

> "When we came in we were told there weren't sufficient inducements to invest. So we provided the inducements. Then we were told people were scared of balance of payments difficulties leading to stop-go. So we floated the pound. Then we were told of fears of inflation: and now we're dealing with that. And still you aren't investing enough".
>
> (Source: 'The Director' June 1973.)

But companies' investment will depend, at least partly, on the relationship between interest rates and the rate of return on investment. Over the past three years interest rates have been relatively high and the rate of return on investment has been falling.

8. Britain also differs from her main competitors in how her investment is paid for. If some part of current production is to be devoted to investment, then the whole of current production clearly cannot be swallowed up in consumption. Someone has to forego consumption in order to make resources available for investment in real terms. If industry is to install new plant and machinery and erect new factories these must be paid for somehow. The funds can only come from:

—**Companies:** either from internal sources such as ploughed back profits, or from external sources, principally share issues to raise fresh capital or borrowings from banks and other financial bodies which attract funds from other sectors of the economy.

—**Persons and households:** by refraining from spending all their income, either by *voluntary* saving—possibly in the form of life assurance, savings with a building society, a pension scheme, or building up a bank balance—or by *compulsory* saving through taxation and national insurance deductions.

—**The public sector** (central and local government and public corporations): by absorbing funds from other sectors and devoting them to public investment or as aids to private industry.

—**Overseas:** by a net inflow of funds from abroad, including recycled oil revenues and borrowings on the Euro-currency markets.

9. The striking difference between British companies and their foreign competitors lies in the predominant role of *internally* generated finance as a proportion of total sources of funds used by British firms. Internal funds, including depreciation provisions (which roughly allow for replacement investment) and retained profits, accounted for over 76 per cent of funds raised by larger quoted industrial and commercial companies over the period 1950-72 (Source: Royal Commission on the Distribution of Income and Wealth, Report No. 2 Chpt 8). The importance of internal funds declined somewhat from the late 1960's, companies making greater use of bank borrowing. Over the ten years 1964-73 UK companies' own savings (i.e. retained profits, depreciation and additions to reserves) were sufficient to finance on average almost 90 per cent of total fixed investment. In 1974 that figure fell below 70 per cent (Source: National Income and Expenditure 1964-74, Table 80).

10. A different pattern applies abroad. On average, over the years 1964-68 the UK corporate sector's gross savings were equivalent to 125 per cent of its gross investment. The corresponding proportions for our major competitors were USA 101 per cent, West Germany 90 per cent, Japan 88 per cent and France 84 per cent. Thus our competitors have relied far more on *external* finance. Recent figures suggest that French companies have been able to undertake fixed investment of up to 20 per cent more than their savings and to rely entirely on external finance for their investment in stocks (although the current five-year plan proposes to reduce French industries' dependence on bank lending and to rely more on internal funds). Corresponding figures for West German, Japanese and U.S. companies are 30 per cent more, 62 per cent more and 28 per cent more, respectively (Source: quoted in Yao-Su Hu "National Attitudes and the Financing of Industry" pages 45-6). Clearly in other countries a financial deficit for the company sector (i.e. broadly an excess of investment in fixed assets and stocks over company savings) seems to be accepted as a fact of life, and is financed by the channelling of resources from persons and households to the company sector, through banks and other financial intermediaries.

11. Comparisons of the financial structure of companies here and abroad indicate a pervasive attitude of conservatism in both our industrial and financial systems. This may go far to explain British industry's poor investment performance. Thus in the 1960's

British companies maintained a significantly smaller ratio between medium and longer-term borrowing on the one hand and retained profits and other shareholders' funds on the other. The UK ratio during the period 1964-68 was 23 per cent, two-thirds the figure for France, half that of West Germany, and only one quarter that of Japan. (Source: Samuels Groves & Goddard op cit page 25). Evidence presented to the Royal Commission on the Distribution of Income and Wealth, from both providers and users of finance, led it to observe that there were levels in this "gearing ratio" between capital with a fixed prior charge on profits and capital such as shares with no guaranteed return, above which it was imprudent for companies to go:

> "We were told that the constraint was imposed by investors who would refrain from holding shares in companies whose gearing was too high, by lenders who would not lend in such circumstances and by company managers who appreciated this and the risks that high gearing brought to their own livelihood".
> (Source: Royal Commission on the Distribution of Income and Wealth, op cit, paragraph 194).

12. The evidence certainly suggests that it is relatively easier for our competitors to raise external finance on a medium to long-term basis than it is for British companies. Similarly creditors and banks who make short-term loans to companies in France and West Germany seem to require relatively less short-term security, as measured by the "acid test" of a company's cash and near-cash assets as a proportion of its current liabilities, than their British counterparts. UK companies therefore have to provide greater cover than their competitors before they can attract short-term funds.

13. The capital structure of companies also suggests that those who lend medium and long-term funds to industry in Britain require that the company could repay the loan from its internal funds much sooner than is required abroad. Thus in the 1960's for every £1 of self-financing British companies borrowed medium or long-term only some four-fifths of the amount their French and West German competitors could, and only half that of Japanese companies (Source: Samuels Groves & Goddard, op cit, page 25).

The Importance of the Financial Institutions

14. How are the savings of the personal sector, which constitute foreign industry's major source of external finance and which pay for the higher levels of corporate investment that we wish to emulate, channelled into manufacturing industry? What is happening to the vast volume of personal saving conducted in Britain? After all, saving as a proportion of personal disposable income in UK has increased by more than half in the past decade, equivalent

to 'extra' savings in 1974 of almost £3000 million (Source: National Income and Expenditure 1964-74 page 26). The answers to these questions indicate the different pattern of saving between Britain and her major competitors, the powerful position of our banks and financial institutions, and the extent to which our competitors have used public ownership within their financial systems to channel resources into industry.

15. One of the major competitors for funds constituting personal savings of one kind or another is, of course, the Government itself. In 1975, a year when public sector borrowing was particularly high, the Government borrowed from the insurance companies £1600 million out of total net investment by them of £2500 million. That is to say about 64 per cent of all insurance company funds went into British Government securities. In the case of pension funds the proportion was somewhat lower, £930 million out of nearly £2500 million, i.e. 38 per cent of all pension fund investments. But these proportions fluctuate considerably from year to year. In 1974 they were only 6 per cent for insurance companies and 5 per cent for pension funds. Over the past five years the proportion has averaged about 20 per cent in each case, representing £550 million per annum in total (Source: Financial Statistics, Business Monitor M5 First Quarter 1976).

16. The personal sector is the most important primary lender of funds to the rest of the economy. But in Britain we have a number of institutions (principally the insurance companies, pension funds, and building societies) which perform functions normally handled abroad by banks. For example in 1973:

* **Banks** attracted some 43 per cent of households' financial savings in Britain compared with 50 per cent in West Germany and 85 per cent in France.
* **Insurance companies and pension funds** attracted 35 per cent of these savings in Britain, compared with 18 per cent in West Germany. Life assurance attracted only $3\frac{1}{2}$ per cent of household's financial savings in France.

(Source: Yao Su-Hu op cit, pages 70-71).

17. A very large proportion of total personal saving in Britain is done on a regular contractual basis in the form of contributions to pension schemes, premiums on life assurance policies, repayment of house purchase loans and the like. Contractual saving through life assurance and pension schemes and mortgage repayments accounted for two-thirds of the estimated increase in total personal saving in the first half of the 1960's. (Source: L. S. Berman "A Note on Contractual Saving in the United Kingdom", Economic Trends August 1967).

18. In 1974 the pattern of personal sector saving and investment was broadly as follows:—

Personal Sector Saving 1974

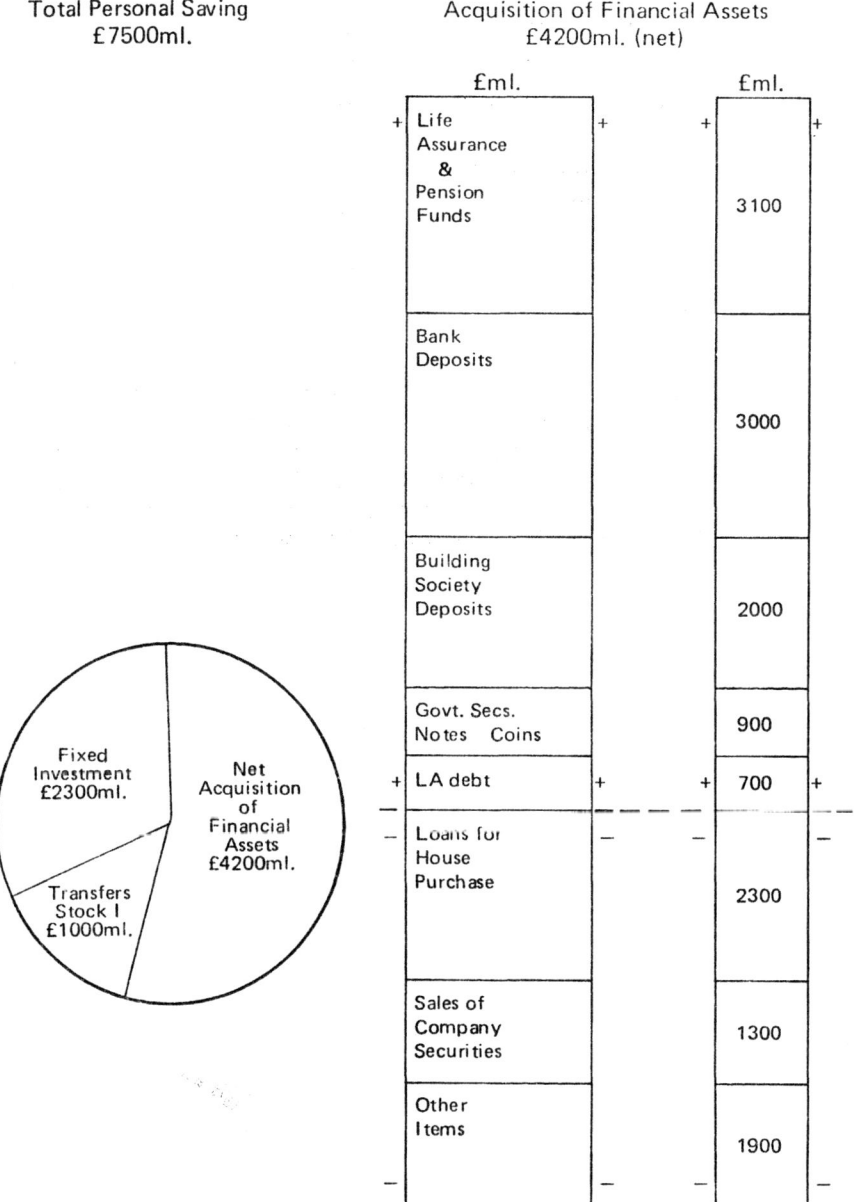

Total Personal Saving
£7500ml.

Acquisition of Financial Assets
£4200ml. (net)

(Source: National Income and Expenditure 1964-74, Table 81).

19. Estimates of financial institutions' contribution to domestic financing (i.e. their purchases of domestic financial assets) in 1967-70 show the following:

	%
Banking Sector	22
Building Societies	32
Insurance Companies	24
Pension Funds	17
Investment trusts & Unit Trusts	5
	100

(Source: J. Revell "Financial Structure and Government Regulation in the United Kingdom 1952-80" page 5).

20. Clearly the financial institutions wield a massive amount of financial power. One area where this is reflected is in the *ownership* of industry. Estimates of the proportion of UK quoted ordinary shares owned by the institutions and by persons indicate a marked decline in direct share ownership by individuals, with institutional holdings roughly doubling over the past twenty years.

Ownership of UK Quoted Ordinary Shares 1957-73

1957	1969	1973
Persons 66%	Persons 47%	Persons 50%
	Insurance 12.2%	Insurance Companies 16.9%
	Pension Funds 9.0%	
Insurance 8.8%	Investment & Unit Trusts 10.5%	Pension Funds 14.6%
Pensions 3.4%	Banks 1.7%	
Investment & Unit Trusts 5.7%		Unit Trusts 4.1%*
Banks 0.9%		
Others 16%	Others 21%	Others 14.4%

* Unit Trusts only

(Sources: J. Moyle "The Pattern of Ordinary Share Ownership 1957-70" Royal Commission on the Distribution of Income and Wealth, op cit, Table 11).

21. The enormous financial power conferred by control over a massive flow of funds is not spread evenly throughout the financial system, but is concentrated amongst a handful of major banks and insurance companies.

* The four major London clearing banks (Barclays, Lloyds, Midland and National Westminster) handle over 90 per cent of the current and deposit accounts of the private London clearers and, with their many subsidiaries, dominate the whole range of banking services. Of the six biggest finance houses controlling over half of all hire purchase business, three are controlled by the "big four" banks.

* Just two companies, Commercial Union and Royal, received almost one quarter of total premiums and over one-third of general premiums (i.e. fire, accident, motor and marine insurance) accruing to British insurance companies in 1974.

* The top six insurance companies accounted for *half* of all premiums and *two-thirds* of general premiums.

(Source: Policy Holder Insurance Journal, October 1975).

The Performance of the Financial System

22. There are four reasons why the manner in which the financial institutions have exercised stewardship of the funds in their care must be questioned.

(1) Investment and Lending Policies

23. In their search for what they regard as "profitable investment opportunities" Britain's financiers have come up with questionable priorities. Institutional purchases of works of art and of agricultural land as "inflation-hedges" do nothing to restore the industrial base on which future prosperity, real incomes and pensions depend. Yet in the quarter ending April 1976 30 per cent of agricultural land purchases were by institutional investors (Source: Country Land-owners Association).

24. The spectacular property boom of 1972-73 was fuelled by funds provided by the insurance companies and pension funds, but most notably by a massive increase in bank lending. In the 12 months following the August 1972 explicit request from the Governor of the Bank of England for banks to restrain their lending to property companies, the total value of clearing banks' outstanding advances rose by 38 per cent. Their lending to manufacturing industry rose by only half this rate at 19 per cent. But loans to property companies jumped by over 75 per cent (Source: Financial Statistics).

25. Similarly over 26 per cent of the net investment of the long term funds of insurance companies belonging to the British Insurance

Association went to land, property and ground rents in the three years 1972-74, i.e. over £800 million, (over £440 million in 1974 alone). This was on top of an increase in bank lending to property companies of £2,200 million between 1971 and 1974. The real total of property borrowings from the banks may have reached more than £5,000 million at the peak, with the sharpest increase in lending coming from the secondary banks given a freer reign by the Tory Government's 'Competition & Credit Control' policy change of 1971 (Source: P. Riddell in the 'Banker' February 1975).

26. When the boom burst the capital values of properties plunged by about half in some cases. Since these properties constituted the security covering the vast over-commitment of bank lending, it was not only the property world that was exposed. The relative success of the Bank of England and clearing banks' "life-boat" operation to prevent a cascade of fringe bank collapses cannot disguise a very real threat to confidence in the whole financial system. The intention to limit the price tag on the "lifeboat" to £1,200 million is an inadequate measure of the size of this threat.

(2) Instability of Institutional Dealing

27. The increasing institutionalisation of funds in the capital market has coincided with more exaggerated cycles in share prices (NEDO, op cit, page 115). Institutional purchase of equities has also followed a violently cyclical pattern, the rate of net acquisition of ordinary shares by insurance companies, pension funds, and investment and unit trusts dropping by over £2,000 million per year between 1972 and 1974. This prompts the question of whether the people whose funds are lodged with institutions are being served sensibly, even in the sense of narrow self-interest. Thus the insurance companies are judged to have sold in the final quarter of 1974 the same volume of shares that they purchased in the third quarter of 1972 at three times their 1974 price, the end result for policy holders being a loss of more than £100 million (Source: John Hughes "Funds for Investment" page 7).

(3) The Significance of the Stock Exchange

"When the capital development of a country becomes a by-product of the activities of a casino, the job is likely to be ill-done".
J. M. Keynes "The General Theory of Employment, Interest and Money", Chap. 12.

28. A particular question mark hangs over the role of the Stock Exchange both in its primary function as a source of new risk capital, and in its secondary function as a market in existing securities. In recent years it has degenerated to barely even a marginal source of new funds. The recovery of capital issues in 1975 may

have repaired its image a little, but most of these funds appear to have been devoted to adjustments to company balance sheets. Indeed in recent years many capital issues were not made to raise new funds at all, but formed part of mergers and takeover bids. Rights issues had been made until recently as a device for getting round dividend controls. Non new-money issues have been of great importance, and even where issues for cash have occurred the object has often been to use the new money to reduce bank borrowing. Thus a need for new funds to finance investment was the motive behind only a few of the companies which made capital issues in 1975 ("The Banker" City of London Survey, February 1976).

29. The suggestion in the recent NEDO report (op cit, page 133) that "The City in general, while concerned with both primary and secondary markets finds the secondary much more remunerative" may help to explain the sensitivity of City interests to suggestions that improvements could be introduced into traditional methods of raising finance for industry, and that the financial community could do more for the nation. Yet the City has still to answer the charge that an overactive secondary market is actually holding industry back, by forcing companies to justify their share price every single day in conditions of increasingly extreme cycles in average share prices, thereby compelling industrialists to restrict their horizons only to projects with relatively short pay-off terms. In France and West Germany companies rely far more on medium and long term loans from banks. In Britain medium and long term finance is harder to attract, as we noted earlier, though approximately 40 per cent of lending by the London clearing banks and their subsidiaries to manufacturing industry is now medium-term. Whilst the insurance companies are extensive purchasers of company securities, little of the funds involved finds it way to industrial companies.

(4) Secrecy

30. An outstanding characteristic of the investment protection committees of the institutional associations is their *secrecy*. Despite the fact that it controls thousands of millions of £'s of workers' deferred pay, the investment protection committee of the National Association of Pension Funds refuses to disclose any details of its work, even the number of its members and how they are elected. Indeed its Secretary is on record as denying that it has any responsibility to the public at all (Source: 'Guardian' 6 October 1975). The Institutional Shareholders' Committee set up on the prompting of the Governor of the Bank of England in 1973 is also surrounded in secrecy, on the insistence of the institutions.

The Relevance of Public Ownership: Lessons from Abroad

31. Britain's past record of comparative failure matters less than the question of its future performance. If we are to double our annual rate of manufacturing investment we must accept that this implies changes in the extent to which industry relies on external funds, and in the mix of external funds. Therefore we must set in hand the institutional reforms necessary to channel resources into industry. One immediate lesson must be learned—"The speculative property boom of 1971-73 demonstrated clearly that to make funds available for investment will not necessarily promote investment in the desired areas" (Investors Chronicle, "The City & Industry").

32. The key to success lies in developing a publicly-owned stake in the very areas of the financial system where critical investment and lending decisions are made: the banks and the insurance companies. This is where our competitors have stolen a march on us, with specialist publicly-owned financial intermediaries.

33. In *France* public and semi-public financial institutions handle about 85 per cent of total bank deposits, giving the French Government tremendous influence over the funds available to finance investment. The three largest commercial banks (Credit Lyonnais, Banque Nationale de Paris, and Societe Generale) are publicly-owned as are three of the biggest insurance companies. Credit Lyonnais, with the largest number of individual, as opposed to business clients, has $4\frac{1}{2}$ million accounts, nearly 2,500 branches and almost 50,000 employees. Banque Nationale de Paris was the biggest EEC bank in terms of net assets in 1974. All three compete amongst themselves, as well as against banks in the private sector.

34. Credit National is a semi-public bank, owned by various financial institutions but with a chairman and senior managers appointed by the Government with whom it acts in close liaison (Yao Su-Hu, op cit, page 24). There is also the Caisse de Depots et Consigrations (CDC) which collects the funds of the French savings banks and insurance companies for investment in public and private company securities, in loans to local authorities, and in housing and public works projects. The CDC therefore occupies a key position as a collector of savings.

35. The *Japanese* equivalent of the French CDC is the Trust Fund Bureau. A major part of all savings and life insurance collected through Japan's 20,000 post offices is deposited with it, and subsequently distributed to government financial institutions, in accordance with a Government investment and loan programme. In addition 12 financial institutions are publicly-owned, and in 1975 they contributed more to the net increase in industrial funds than the entire private sector. The most important of these 12 is the Japan Development Bank which supplies medium and longer-term funds to firms in the chemicals, machinery, electric power, steel, coalmining and shipping sectors. Loans must be used for the acquisition, modernisation and rationalisation of plant and equipment, and are generally made in conjunction with finance from private institutions. In addition Japan's life assurance companies devote some two-thirds of their operating assets to loans mostly for industrial equipment, and only one-third to securities (Source: Yao Su-Hu, op cit, page 37).

36. The Japanese industrial and financial systems are especially closely linked through the important part played by the banks in financing the 10 massive commercial and trading conglomerates which dominate the Japanese economy. These 10 SOGOSHOSHA account for half Japan's exports, almost two-thirds of her imports, and one-fifth of domestic wholesaling.

37. In *Italy* the IRI state holding company owns three of the largest banks, and has holdings in a number of local banks. The six other joint stock banks are also publicly-owned. The result is that Government has direct or indirect control over half the deposits in Italian Banks. This control is heightened by a number of special credit institutions which are owned by IRI or by one of the nationalised banks.

38. The principal form of bank in *West Germany* is publicly-owned and organised in a national co-operative. *Belgium's* largest bank is publicly-owned, and there is a sizeable co-operative sector. Co-operative banking also plays a vital role in the banking systems of *Denmark* and the *Netherlands*. Whilst Britain has a vigorously competitive and expanding Co-operative Bank, which is breaking new ground in being accepted as a member of the Bankers Clearing House, it still accounts for only 1 per cent of deposits in deposit banks. Thus, taken as a whole Britain's banking system appears out of step with Japan and the rest of Europe. Since British insurance companies perform functions which on the continent are mainly handled by banks, public ownership is clearly also relevant to them.

Programme of Reform

39. The Government has already taken some action to aid the process of steering funds into productive investment. The Price Code has been relaxed to boost company profitability; public funds have been made available under the Industry Act; arrangements have been made to increase to £1,000 million the financing capability of Finance For Industry, the agency which is jointly owned by the Bank of England and the clearing banks, and which is intended to provide longer term funds to industry from funds made available by the banks, insurance companies and pension funds. The original intention was that FFI should lend £1,000 million over a two year period, most of that to be allocated by the end of 1975-76. In fact FFI loan commitments are still only in the region of £200 million (The Bankers' Magazine, May 1976.) Talks are proceeding into the possibility of making banks' medium term loans to industry qualify for refinancing at the Bank of England. Finally, Equity Capital For Industry has been launched by the City to channel funds to viable companies unable to raise finance elsewhere in the capital market. Original discussions were in terms of possibly £500 million being made available, but in the event the insurance companies, pension funds, investment trusts and unit trusts have agreed to subscribe less than £50 million, a relatively insignificant sum compared with the total value of funds that industry will require if investment does recover.

40. These are highly laudable innovations. But we do not believe they go far enough, soon enough, to exploit the scope that undoubtedly exists for new institutions charged with channelling funds into industry. For example the £1,000 million capability intended for FFI contrasts with the £2,000 million plus which France's CDC is able to lend in a year. Accordingly we propose that further steps be taken.

(1) An Investment Reserve Fund

41. Companies should be encouraged to plough a proportion of their funds into an investment reserve fund, releases from which would be supervised by a reformed Bank of England and conditional upon being devoted to productive investment. Based upon the Swedish scheme, but adapted to UK requirements, this could involve Category I companies with large "blocked balances" at the Bank of England, earning no interest at all and available only for investment agreed through the Planning Agreements System. By earmarking a proportion of firms' pre-tax profits in this way, and by reducing the "opportunity cost" of investment (e.g. the high interest rates which the "blocked" funds could otherwise attract in the money market) the attraction of investment projects at the margin could be enhanced sufficiently for them to be given the go-ahead. Favourable treatment could perhaps be given to participating companies in access to external funds, possibly in the form of subsidised interest rates. A Government subsidy of £500 million would enable the interest rate paid by companies on £1,000 million of medium term loans to be reduced by two-thirds, from about 15 per cent to about 5 per cent (P. Readman in the 'Guardian' 14 June 1976).

(2) Integration of the Existing Public Sector

42. In 1975 the National Savings Bank and National Giro, both of which attract funds through the Post Office branch network, handled deposits of £2,200 million between them. Giro is still very much in its infancy and provides a money-transfer service to its customers. Both the Post Office Engineering Union, in evidence to the Post Office Review Committee, and the Post Office Board Member responsible for Giro have recently suggested that Giro be combined with the National Savings Bank and the Paymaster General's office to form a major state bank. This proposal has many attractions. Whether or not the Trustee Savings Banks, which have recently undergone major changes in their role, should also participate warrants further consideration. But we endorse the remainder of the proposal and would welcome discussion with representatives of the staffs involved, to hear their views and to ensure their interests are safeguarded.

(3) Public Ownership of the Major Banks and Insurance Companies

43. We are convinced that the public authorities in Britain must become as involved in banking and insurance as are their counterparts in France and many other leading industrial nations. A major extension of public ownership in these fields could facilitate a significant improvement in services to customers, especially to policy-holders with insurance companies, without necessitating a total monopoly approach that would serve the interests of neither customers nor staff. It would also provide the instruments the British economy needs for ensuring that the financial and industrial systems operate in harmony, jointly promoting the communal interest by ensuring that savers' funds go to support the industrial investment on which jobs and real incomes depend in the long-term, instead of being siphoned off into speculative property ventures and the like. This would promote the interest of savers, depositors, borrowers, and investors alike far more than the smooth sales talk and blinkered outlook of those city "whizz-kids" who are able, at present, so to manipulate other people's money as to make the value of the headquarters buildings of major industrial concerns appear to be worth more than the value of the concern itself as a provider of jobs and exports.

Insurance

44. We propose that the top seven insurance companies (Commercial Union, Royal, Prudential, Guardian Royal Exchange, General Accident, Sun Alliance & London, and Legal and General) be brought into public ownership and placed under the control of a reformed Bank of England. This would establish public control over more than half of total premium income and over two-thirds of British insurance companies' general funds. It would also bring a substantial part of motor insurance into the public sector with consequential improvements to the security of thousands of motorists.

45. Seven major bankruptcies in as many years—robbing $1\frac{1}{2}$ million motorists of cover—demonstrate a serious need for reform of motor insurance. The case for a full-scale review is made especially compelling by the very high proportion of gross premiums absorbed by commissions and administrative costs (over 30 per cent in 1970 compared with the 5 per cent which administrative costs represented of National Insurance contributions), and by the fact that third party liability insurance is compulsory for all drivers and directly affects many more people. We also feel that further study should be made into "no fault" liability motor insurance, which appears to be highly successful in Canada and many American states in saving administration costs as well as ensuring that all victims of accidents do receive compensation without needing to prove liability of a party to the accident. New Zealand has perhaps the most comprehensive no-fault motor insurance scheme, financed by an annual levy on drivers' licences. This possibility, or of a levy on petrol or on road fund licence, should also be examined.

Banking

46. We propose that the big four private clearing banks be brought into public ownership, together with a merchant bank. In view of the diversity of customers' requirements, their legitimate interest in choice, and of French experience of competition amongst her three major publicly-owned commercial banks, the separate identities of Britain's biggest clearing banks should be maintained. This would also eliminate any possibility of disruption of working arrangements and responsibilities which might otherwise flow from nationalisation, in the interests of customers and staff alike. These banks should be placed under Bank of England control, which should act as a holding company and plan the provision of bank finance to industry.

47. It could be argued that the Government already has all the powers it needs to control the banking system, through directives issued under the 1946 Bank of England Act. In practice no such directives have ever been issued. All our experience of managing the 'mixed economy' demonstrates that there is no substitute for public ownership when it comes to engineering a radical change in attitudes to investment priorities. If only a single clearing bank were brought into public ownership there would exist a possibility of deposits being switched, for misguided reasons, to the other clearers. This would not only render the act of nationalisation futile but increase even more the dominance of what would become the "Big Three". So the public stake in banking must be substantial to prove viable. Taking over the "Big Four" is the obvious course.

(4) Reform of the Bank of England

48. The Bank of England was nationalised 30 years ago. It has yet to be socialised. The 1970 Report of the Select Committee on Nationalised Industries laid bare the lack of public accountability of the Bank at that time. Some steps have been taken since 1970 to unveil the shroud of secrecy with which the Bank long shielded its affairs, even from the Treasury. Since 1971 the Bank has published audited accounts along with its annual report, which is presented to Parliament by the Chancellor of the Exchequer. Its capital spending is now subject to a process of analysis and discussion similar to that which applies to the nationalised industries. The Government receives the full profits of the Issue Department of the Bank. But the Bank's unofficial role as representative to Government of City interests persists to this day, and continues to generate public suspicion of undue political influence.

49. A distinct break must be made in the role played by the Bank of England. In future its enormous resources must be brought to bear in support of the Government's industrial strategy as well as its overall economic policy. The Bank must contribute to industrial planning working with the high level National Planning Commission proposed in "Labour's Programme 1976". We are still considering precise working arrangements but, as proposed above, the Bank should be given responsibility for the Investment Reserve Fund Scheme, for the publicly-owned sections of banking and insurance, and for planning the provision of finance to industry.

50. To assist further in channelling funds from private sector financial institutions to industry a special division, or agency, of the Bank should be established. Through this, bodies such as pension funds could invest long-term funds (backed by Government guarantee), possibly through the purchase of special bonds issued for this purpose by the Bank. But the private sector institutions should not be obliged to invest in such bonds. We would thus have created two sectors within the financial system: one publicly-owned and able to exert a decisive influence over the channelling of funds to industrial investment; the second privately owned, and filling a subordinate but still crucial role in controlling the flow of funds within the economy.

Summary and Conclusion

51. For too long the financial system has been able to shelter behind a mystique of its own creation. That mystique has finally been punctured by the extent of the threat to confidence and to people's savings from a series of failures which now compel serious questioning of the operations of the financial system. The "difficulties" experienced by second mortgage specialists Cedar Holdings and First National Finance; by finance houses Moorgate Mercantile, United Dominion Trust, Mercantile Credit and Lombard North Central; by London and County Securities, Western Credit, Keyser Ullman and Cannon Street Investments; the failures of Vehicle and General, Bastion Insurance, London Indemnity and General Insurance, and Nation Life Insurance; and the current problems of merchant bankers Edward Bates all suggest that the 1967 Companies Act, the 1973 Insurance Companies Amendment Act etc. were nowhere near tough enough to safeguard the public. We must now recognise the commanding heights of the economy for what they are, and acknowledge that a major publicly-owned stake in banking and insurance is an essential condition for a viable economic strategy and for sustained recovery.

52. Our experience of industry and the financial system teaches us that we would be unwise either to wait upon their lead, or to passively accept the pace they adopt or to blindly follow in the direction they set. Accordingly this Statement proposes:—

* A publicly-controlled Investment Reserve Fund Scheme to encourage firms to invest, as suggested in our 1975 Statement "Labour and Industry".
* Integration of the existing publicly-owned sections of the financial system by combining the Giro and National Savings Movement.

* A major publicly-owned stake in the financial system comprising the top seven insurance companies, (sufficient to account for 50 per cent of total premium income) a merchant bank and the four major private clearing banks, whose separate identities, services to customers and responsibilities to staff would be maintained.

* Reform of the Bank of England so that it ceases to be the spokesman for the private sector financial institutions and takes on responsibility for the investment fund scheme, for publicly-owned banking and insurance, and for co-ordinating and planning the provision of finance to industry.

53. It is essential that all sections of the Labour Movement, especially the unions representing banking and insurance staff, give voice to their feelings on these issues. The spokesmen of financial interests are already congratulating themselves on having survived the collapse of the property boom and its aftermath, conveniently forgetting the City's original escape into unreality. For 25 years the Doctrine of the Unripe Time has been used as an excuse for refusing to grasp the nettle. The lack of any outright commitment in Labour's October 1974 Manifesto other than "to ensure that banking and insurance make a better contribution to the national economy" need not prevent the Annual Conference from adding to the Party's official policy Programme. In doing so Conference should be aware of the extensive influence of bankers and financiers anxious to preserve the 'status quo', and their own privileged place within it, by claims that despite the evidence, all is for the best in the best of all possible financial worlds.

The Spokesman
Complicity against Palestine
Edited by Tony Simpson

**Published by Spokesman for the
Bertrand Russell Peace Foundation
Ken Coates: Editor from 1970 to 2010**

Spokesman 111　　　　　　　　　**2011**

CONTENTS

Cover: Bethlehem – illegally walled up (Leila)

ISSN 1367 7748　　Printed by the Russell Press Ltd., Nottingham, UK　　ISBN 978 0 85124 790 8

Subscriptions
Institutions £35.00
Individuals £20.00 (UK)
　　　　　£25.00 (ex UK)

Back issues available
on request

A CIP catalogue record
for this book is available
from the British Library

Published by the
Bertrand Russell Peace
Foundation Ltd.,
Russell House
Bulwell Lane
Nottingham NG6 0BT
England
Tel. 0115 9784504
email:
elfeuro@compuserve.com
www.spokesmanbooks.com
www.russfound.org

FSC
Mixed Sources
Product group from well-managed
forests and other controlled sources

Cert no. SGS-COC-006541
www.fsc.org
© 1996 Forest Stewardship Council

Unite - London & Eastern Region

Woodberry
218 Green Lanes
London
N4 2HB

www.unitetheunion.org.uk

End the aggression in Gaza

Justice for the Palestinians

Solidarity with the PGFTU

Steve Hart - Regional Secretary   *Jim Kelly - Regional Chair*